INSIDE THE NBA

ATLANTA HAWKS

BY ANTHONY K. HEWSON

SportsZone
An Imprint of Abdo Publishing
abdobooks.com

abdobooks.com

Published by Abdo Publishing, a division of ABDO, PO Box 398166, Minneapolis, Minnesota 55439.

Printed in China.
052022
092022

THIS BOOK CONTAINS RECYCLED MATERIALS

Cover Photo: Kevin C. Cox/Getty Images Sport/Getty Images
Interior Photos: Melinda Nagy/Shutterstock Images, 1; Tony Dejak/AP Images, 4; Mike Lawrie/Getty Images Sport/Getty Images, 7; Kevin C. Cox/Getty Images Sport/Getty Images, 8, 39, 41; Matt Slocum/AP Images, 9; Tim Nwachukwu/Getty Images Sport/Getty Images, 11; Bettman/Getty Images, 12, 34; Jack Zehrt/FPG/Archive Photos/Getty Images, 15; Focus on Sport/Getty Images, 18, 24, 33; Mitchell Layton/Getty Images Sport/Getty Images, 19; Kevork Djansezian/Getty Images Sport/Getty Images, 20; Curtis Compton/Atlanta Journal-Constitution/AP Images, 21; Wendell Cruz/Pool USA Today Sports/AP Images, 23; Focus on Sport/Getty Images Sport/Getty Images, 27; Sporting News/Getty Images, 28; Hans Deryk/AP Images, 29; Clive Brunskill /Allsport/Getty Images Sport/Getty Images, 31; Stephen Dunn /Allsport/Getty Images Sport/Getty Images, 37

Editor: Charlie Beattie
Series Designer: Joshua Olson

Library of Congress Control Number: 2021951674

Publisher's Cataloging-in-Publication Data

Names: Hewson, Anthony K., author.
Title: Atlanta Hawks / by Anthony K. Hewson
Description: Minneapolis, Minnesota: Abdo Publishing, 2023 | Series: Inside the NBA | Includes online resources and index.
Identifiers: ISBN 9781532198182 (lib. bdg.) | ISBN 9781098271831 (ebook)
Subjects: LCSH: Atlanta Hawks (Basketball team)--Juvenile literature. | Basketball--Juvenile literature. | Professional sports--Juvenile literature. | Sports franchises--Juvenile literature.
Classification: DDC 796.32364--dc23

TABLE OF CONTENTS

GEEK
sharecare
ATLANTA
11

CHAPTER ONE

FOREVER YOUNG

Trae Young stopped his run to set up behind the three-point line. Just then, a freight train named Dwight Howard ran into him from behind. The massive, 6-foot-10-inch Philadelphia 76ers center flattened Atlanta's star point guard. At 6-foot-1 and 164 pounds, Young is hardly a big National Basketball Association (NBA) player. The situation didn't look great as Young lay on his stomach on the court. Then he hopped right up and did a few pushups.

Young was having some fun in a tense moment of a big game. It was Game 7 of the 2021 Eastern Conference semifinals. Young's Hawks were tied with the 76ers midway through the second quarter. Yet Young seemed hardly fazed by the moment. The 22-year-old calmly stepped up to the line and made two free throws to give Atlanta a two-point lead.

Trae Young goes up for a jumper against the Cleveland Cavaliers in December 2021.

The game wasn't coming as easily to Young as he made it look in that moment, though. He had made just one field goal in the half.

TEAM EFFORT

Young was the team's star. But if the Hawks were going to win, they were going to need everyone. Atlanta had a tight-knit team. They'd been playing together for a few years. Power forward John Collins was Atlanta's first-round draft pick in 2017. Young was the fifth overall pick in the 2018 draft by the Dallas Mavericks. He came to the Hawks on draft night in a trade for Luka Dončić. Shooting guard Kevin Huerter was chosen later in that same round. During those first few years, the Hawks didn't do much winning. They needed some help. Ahead of the 2020–21 season, they got some veteran players like center Clint Capela and guard Bogdan Bogdanović.

There was no doubt, though, that Young was the team's driving force. He was coming off his first season as an All-Star starter. In 2019–20 he had averaged nearly 30 points per game. But the Hawks had won just 20 games. When Atlanta started 14–20 in 2020–21, it looked like another development year for the Hawks. Things clicked for the team after that. The Hawks finished 27–11. Then Young starred as they knocked off the New York Knicks in the first round of the playoffs. Fans wondered if he could do it again and move Atlanta to the Eastern Conference finals.

Young, *far left*, led the country in scoring during his only season at the University of Oklahoma before he was drafted fifth overall in 2018.

BACK AND FORTH IN PHILADELPHIA

The teams had traded momentum throughout the series. Atlanta won a tight game, 128–124, in Game 1. Philadelphia answered with back-to-back blowouts behind star center Joel Embiid. But Young answered back for the Hawks. He led them to three-point victories in Games 4 and 5. A 104–99 Philadelphia win in Game 6 forced a decisive matchup.

Now the teams were locked in yet another tight game. The Hawks took a two-point halftime lead over the 76ers. The Philadelphia crowd was hoping their team would soon overwhelm the young Hawks. But Atlanta had other ideas.

Young was the Hawks' leading scorer in six of the seven games against Philadelphia.

The teams traded the lead eight times in the third quarter. Young still wasn't scoring. But he found other ways to put points on the board. Early in the quarter, Young found Capela open for dunks three times in just over two minutes. With 57 seconds left, Young dished out another pass. This time Collins slammed it home to give Atlanta a 72–69 lead. Atlanta took a five-point edge into the fourth quarter.

Atlanta struggled on offense when the final quarter started. The Hawks didn't hit a field goal until forward Danilo Gallinari hit a three-pointer nearly five minutes in. But Atlanta was holding its own on defense. Gallinari's shot cut the lead to one, 81–80.

As the teams traded baskets, quick shots from Young and Huerter tied the game at 84–84 with 5:55 left. On the next Atlanta possession, Young dribbled outside the three-point line. He put a move on a defender and drove to the hoop. He jumped and released a floating shot high in the air. It dropped through the rim for an Atlanta lead.

Hawks forward Danilo Gallinari powers home the dunk that put Game 7 away.

The Hawks held a one-point lead with just over three minutes left. Young brought the ball up court and drove to the hoop. He had plenty of room to put up his own shot. Instead he spied Capela waiting near the basket. Young lobbed up a pass for him, and Capela slammed home a dunk.

PULLING AWAY

While still dishing out assists, Young also found his shooting touch late in the game. On the next possession after Capela's dunk, Young was dribbling well beyond the three-point arc.

He sized up a shot and let it go from 29 feet. It hit nothing but net, and the Hawks had their biggest lead of the quarter, 93–87.

The 76ers still refused to go away. Two layups and a free throw cut Atlanta's lead back to one as the game entered its final minute. Huerter dribbled up the floor and came around a Capela screen at the three-point line. As Huerter hoisted a three-point shot, Philadelphia's Matisse Thybulle charged around the screen. Thybulle lunged to block Huerter's shot. Instead he tapped the Atlanta guard's arm. Huerter already had 24 points. Now he stepped to the line for three free throws. After he knocked them down, Atlanta was in control again. Whatever the 76ers tried, the Hawks had an answer.

It was Gallinari who provided the final blow. Embiid tried to dribble around Gallinari at the top of the key on the next possession. As he spun in the lane, Embiid lost the handle on the ball. It flew right into Huerter's hands in the corner. By the time he picked it up, Gallinari was halfway up the

A Great Series

Game 7 was Young's fifth double-double of the series. But it was far from his most impressive. Atlanta entered Game 4 at home trailing the series 2–1. In the Hawks' 103–100 victory, Young piled up 25 points but also dished out 18 assists. That total tied a career high. Young averaged 29.0 points and 10.9 assists in the seven games.

Hawks' guard Bogdan Bogdanović attempts to silence the Philadelphia crowd late in the fourth quarter of Game 7.

floor. Huerter hit him in stride, and Gallinari flushed home a game-clinching dunk.

After the clock hit zero, Young took his jersey off and ran into the stands. He tossed it to his dad, who pumped his fist in celebration. Young had a poor shooting game, just 5-for-23. But he scored 10 of his 21 points in the decisive final quarter. The point guard also added 10 assists. More importantly, the Hawks had just won a Game 7 on the road for the first time in their history. And Young had led them there. Fans couldn't wait to see what he could do next.

HAWKS
16
F

CHAPTER TWO

LONG ROAD TO ATLANTA

The Buffalo Bisons struggled to draw crowds in their first season in the National Basketball League (NBL). It wasn't because they had poor players. The 1946–47 Bisons had Dan Otten, one of few players back then who stood 7 feet tall. They also had William "Pop" Gates, a future Hall of Famer who was one of the first Black professional basketball stars. But even with ticket prices at just one dollar, it was tough to fill the seats at Buffalo Memorial Auditorium in western New York.

Just about 1,000 fans showed up to the game on December 16, 1946. The Bisons then left on a road trip. They never played another game in Buffalo. On December 25, general manager Leo Farris announced the Bisons were moving to Moline, Illinois.

Once they got there, the team was renamed the Tri-Cities Blackhawks. Moline was part of a three-city area that included

Cliff Hagan of the St. Louis Hawks drives the baseline against the Detroit Pistons in 1958.

Rock Island, Illinois, and Davenport, Iowa. The team fared much better in Moline. The Blackhawks made the playoffs in their first three seasons. The 1948–49 season was their best yet. Otten won NBL Most Valuable Player (MVP). The next year, the NBL merged with the Basketball Association of America (BAA). The new league was renamed the NBA. The Blackhawks were one of the new league's original members.

They had a new coach as well. Red Auerbach went 28–29 as head coach that year. After it was over, he resigned. That was the last time Auerbach had a losing record. He took a new job with the Boston Celtics. Auerbach turned the Celtics into the NBA's most successful team. He won nine NBA titles as coach in Boston before retiring to the front office in 1966.

The NBA proved to be a much more popular league than the NBL. However, teams were based mostly in much bigger cities than Moline. With that in mind, Blackhawks owner Ben Kerner moved the team to Milwaukee, Wisconsin, after the 1950–51 season. The team also shortened its nickname to the Hawks.

PETTIT BECOMES A STAR

Milwaukee was also where the team picked up one of its greatest players ever. Bob Pettit was the second pick in the 1954 draft. A center in college, Pettit became a dominant

Bob Pettit (9) attempts a jump shot against the Boston Celtics.

power forward in the NBA. He won Rookie of the Year in 1954–55.

Milwaukee fans got to enjoy Pettit's play for only one season. The team was on the move again before the 1955–56 season. This time it turned up in St. Louis, Missouri. The Hawks would enjoy their longest period of success there.

Pettit won MVP in his first season in St. Louis. The Hawks returned to the playoffs and faced the mighty Minneapolis Lakers. St. Louis won Game 1 by one point. The Lakers then blew them out by 58 points in Game 2. But the Hawks bounced back to win the series before falling in the next round.

The Hawks became one of the top teams in the NBA. Pettit led the way. But he also had key teammates like Ed Macauley, Jack McMahon, and Cliff Hagan. Despite having a losing record of 34–38 in 1956–57, the team still had a chance at the playoffs. Both the Lakers and Fort Wayne Pistons also finished 34–38. The three teams had a series of playoff games to decide the division champion. St. Louis beat the Pistons 115–103 in the first game. Two days later, the Hawks held off the Lakers 114–111. St. Louis had its first division title. St. Louis then beat the Lakers in a three-game playoff series to reach the NBA Finals. However, they fell to Auerbach's Celtics there.

Losing Russell

Ed Macauley and Cliff Hagan were both great players for the Hawks. Each made the Hall of Fame. But the Hawks traded center Bill Russell in a 1956 draft-day deal to get them. Russell went on to lead the Boston Celtics to 11 championships and is considered one of the greatest players of all time.

The 1957–58 Hawks won a team-record 41 games. They got a rematch with the Celtics in the Finals. This time, the Hawks knocked off the champs in six games. Pettit set a playoff record with 50 points in Game 6. But little did they know at the time, St. Louis would be the only team besides Boston to win the NBA title from 1957 through 1966.

Pettit and the Hawks looked as if they would win more titles. Pettit won a second MVP in 1959. The Hawks made it back to the Finals in 1960 and 1961. But they lost to the Celtics both times.

The team remained competitive after that. Pettit had his best scoring season, averaging 31.1 points, in 1961–62. Meanwhile, young point guard Lenny Wilkens and forward Lou Hudson were emerging as new stars. In 1967–68 the team set a team record with 56 wins.

The Hawks seemed to be as successful as they could be. Over 13 seasons in St. Louis, the team missed the playoffs only once. But shortly after that 1967–68 season, owner Ben Kerner announced he had sold the team to new owners from Georgia. Once again the Hawks were a team on the move. They began play in Atlanta the next season.

ON TO ATLANTA

Young scoring sensation "Pistol" Pete Maravich helped the Hawks shine in their new city. He and Hudson were the team's leading scorers in the first few seasons in Atlanta. The Hawks remained a playoff team too. However, they never challenged for a championship.

The Hawks missed the playoffs in 1973–74 for the first time in 12 years. Rumors swirled that the team could be on the move again. But Atlanta businessman Ted Turner bought the team in 1977 and promised to keep it in the Peach State.

Pete Maravich spent the first four seasons of his NBA career in Atlanta before he was traded away in 1974.

Atlanta made a steal of a trade in September 1982. They picked up forward Dominique Wilkins, that summer's third overall pick, from the Utah Jazz. Once in Atlanta, Wilkins became known as the "Human Highlight Film" for his flashy dunks.

Wilkins was one of the NBA's most exciting players. He won dunk contests and led the Hawks to 50 wins or more each season from 1985–86 to 1988–89. He became the team's all-time leading scorer. But the Hawks

Dominique Wilkins dunked his way to 23,292 career points in 12 seasons with the Hawks.

never advanced past the second round of the playoffs during his time with the team.

Wilkins was traded in 1994 as the Hawks revamped their lineup during the mid 1990s. A new signing in 1996 made the biggest difference. Center Dikembe Mutombo was one of the best defensive players in the NBA.

Mutombo joined star guards Mookie Blaylock and Steve Smith. The towering center was named Defensive Player of the

Joe Johnson, *left*, made six All-Star teams in seven years with the Hawks before leaving the team in 2012.

Year in 1997 and 1998. The Hawks won a lot of games. But they still couldn't win in the playoffs. All three players were traded over the next few years.

REBUILDING YEARS

With its stars gone, Atlanta missed the playoffs eight years in a row starting in 1999–2000. During that time, the Hawks completely remade the roster. One key move was a trade for guard Joe Johnson in 2005. The multitalented player helped get the Hawks back on the right track.

Al Horford reacts after hitting a game-winning shot during the 2015 Eastern Conference semifinals against the Washington Wizards.

Johnson teamed up with forwards Al Horford and Josh Smith to give Atlanta an effective lineup. And beginning in 2007–08, the Hawks started a new 10-year playoff streak.

With such a long run, players came and went from Atlanta. Horford and guard Jeff Teague led the team in 2014–15. They were joined by future All-Stars in shooting guard Kyle Korver and power forward Paul Millsap. The Hawks had won just 38 games the year before. But a quick

Retired Numbers

The Hawks have retired six uniform numbers. Five belong to legendary players such as Bob Pettit. But one belongs to former Atlanta mayor Kasim Reed. Reed was a big supporter of the Hawks during his time in office from 2010 to 2018. The team thanked him by retiring No. 59 in 2017. Reed was the fifty-ninth mayor in the city's history.

turnaround set a team record with 60 wins. The Hawks then won two playoff series for the first time since 1958.

That success did not last. The Hawks fell to a record of 24–58 by 2017–18. But that poor record meant they'd score the third overall draft pick. The Hawks used it to select Luka Dončić. He would emerge as one of the NBA's top players. But it wasn't with the Hawks. They immediately traded Dončić for the rights to the fifth overall pick, point guard Trae Young.

Young went to work running the Hawks offense. By 2020 he was starting the All-Star Game. The next year, he led his teammates on a magical run to the conference finals. The Hawks had their newest superstar and hoped a long-awaited championship run was right around the corner.

Trae Young, *left*, and forward John Collins, *right*, emerged as a potent young scoring pair for the Hawks.

Hawks
21
bullets
bullets

CHAPTER THREE

SOARING HAWKS

Bob Pettit didn't just set the standard for great Hawks players. He set the standard for great NBA power forwards.

The NBA was a physical league when Pettit was drafted in 1954. Despite Pettit weighing 200 pounds, some thought he wasn't big and strong enough to be an impact player. But Pettit used hard work and relentless rebounding to be one of the best scorers of his era. He was a star from day one. He was named Rookie of the Year after the 1954–55 season. The next year, he was the NBA's MVP.

Pettit made the All-Star team in every one of his 11 seasons with the Hawks. He led the league in scoring twice and never finished lower than seventh. The Hawks built a winning team around Pettit. And he was at his best in the 1958 NBA Finals. Pettit poured in 50 points in Game 6 as the Hawks won their first NBA title.

Dominique Wilkins (21) goes up for a shot against the Washington Bullets.

Pettit retired in 1965 as the NBA's leading scorer and second-leading rebounder. He was also the first player in league history to score 20,000 points. Though just 32 years old, Pettit had struggled with injuries later in his career. He was elected to the Hall of Fame in 1970.

High-scoring forwards are part of the Hawks history. John Drew didn't get as much attention as some stars. But in the 1970s, there were few better scorers in the NBA. He averaged more than 20 points per game in five of eight Hawks' seasons. Drew was a great ball handler you could count on to lay in a basket.

When it came to soaring to the hoop, no Hawk did it better than Dominique Wilkins. No Hawk scored more points, either. And he almost didn't wind up playing for Atlanta.

Wilkins was a top draft prospect in 1982. The Utah Jazz chose him third overall. But Wilkins did not want to play for Utah. And the Jazz needed money. They agreed to trade Wilkins for $1 million and two players, including Drew.

The 6-foot-8, extremely athletic Wilkins became the Hawks' iconic player from the

Ted Turner

Businessman Ted Turner is one of the most famous people in Atlanta. He is best known for starting the CNN and TBS television networks. He also bought baseball's Atlanta Braves in 1976 and the Hawks in 1977. Turner would sell both teams in the 2000s.

John Drew averaged 21.2 points per game over eight seasons with the Hawks before he was traded in 1982.

Atlanta era. He broke Pettit's scoring record in 1993. Wilkins's scoring average of 24.8 points per game ranked fourteenth in NBA history. But his career was about more than numbers. The "Human Highlight Film" had a huge variety of dunks. But his trademark was a windmill, which he did both one- and two-handed. Wilkins memorably won two dunk contests. The first came against Michael Jordan in 1985.

Dikembe Mutombo made the All-Star team four times in five seasons with the Hawks.

SUPER CENTERS

While Wilkins was soaring to the rim, Wayne "Tree" Rollins was firmly planted on the ground. The 7-foot-1-inch center was a dominant force in the 1970s and 1980s. Fans loved Rollins for his physical play in the paint. He had the most blocks in Hawks history. When he retired from the league, only three players had more blocks.

When it comes to centers, Dikembe Mutombo was as good as they come. Mutombo was already a star when he signed with Atlanta in 1996. He reached new heights as a Hawk, winning two of his four Defensive Player of the Year awards.

Standing 7 feet, 2 inches, Mutombo was almost impossible to shoot over. He blocked more than 1,000 shots as a Hawk, among the more than 3,200 for his career. When Mutombo rejected a shot, he often wagged his finger to remind his opponents of what they could not do.

As tough as he was on the court, Mutombo was known for his kindness off it. Mutombo was from the Democratic Republic of the Congo. During and after his career, he did a lot of charity work back home and throughout Africa.

Center/forward Al Horford joined the Hawks in 2007. Many star players came and went in his nine seasons. But Horford was a steady presence pulling down rebounds. As a threat at both ends of the court, Horford was a big part of the 2014–15 Hawks that won 60 games.

Lenny Wilkens played for the St. Louis Hawks for eight seasons in the 1960s, then coached the Atlanta Hawks to six playoff appearances in the 1990s.

GREAT GUARDS

A point guard's job is to look over the court and run the offense. Because of this, they often make good coaches. Lenny Wilkens was a perfect example. He ran the show as a player for the Hawks from 1960 to 1968. Wilkens averaged 11.7 points per game as a rookie. By his final season in St. Louis, he averaged 20.0 points with 8.3 assists. He finished runner-up for MVP.

Wilkens later returned as Hawks head coach in 1993–94. He immediately transformed the team's defense. The Hawks won 57 games, and Wilkens was named Coach of the Year. Wilkens coached Atlanta for seven seasons. He had a winning record in six of them.

"Sweet Lou" Hudson had the versatility to play guard or forward. That was easy for someone with Hudson's athletic ability. He was selected in both the NBA and National Football League drafts in 1966. And he didn't even play college football.

Basketball was Hudson's calling. He averaged more than 20 points per game in 11 seasons with the Hawks. Starting in 1969–70, Hudson averaged 24 points per game over the next five seasons.

Hudson spent most of his time at forward in the early 1970s. The Hawks had a young legend in the making at guard. "Pistol" Pete Maravich played

Jason Collier's Number

No. 40 is not one of the Hawks' retired numbers. But nobody has worn it since Jason Collier did in 2004–05. Collier died suddenly just before the 2005–06 season from a heart attack. The Hawks did not officially retire the number. But they removed it as an option for any player to wear again, to honor Collier's memory.

Mookie Blaylock, *right*, looks to drive during a game against the Orlando Magic.

only four seasons in Atlanta. But he made his mark on the Hawks with flashy and exciting play.

Not everyone loved the Pistol. Some veteran players didn't like his flashy style. Others were jealous of his nearly $2 million contract. It was the highest in pro sports at the time. But even Maravich's critics had to agree that he put on a show on the court.

Maravich's career was a blend of behind-the-back dribbles and between-the-legs passes. He also was one of the best scorers the NBA had ever seen. Maravich increased his average to 27.7 points per game by 1973–74. He and Hudson formed a dynamic scoring duo. However, Atlanta traded him to the New Orleans Jazz that offseason.

One of the players who benefitted from Lenny Wilkens's defensive coaching style was point guard Mookie Blaylock. Blaylock turned into an offensive and defensive force under Wilkens. He became one of just five players to lead the NBA in steals in back-to-back years. Blaylock was the Hawks' all-time leader in three-pointers when he left the team in 1999.

Players in today's NBA shoot from beyond the arc far more often than when Blaylock played. Point guard Trae Young started playing with the Hawks in 2018. But after his first few seasons, he was already fifth in three-pointers made.

Young is way more than a three-point shooter, though. He can score from anywhere on the floor. And he averaged more than nine assists per game in two of his first three NBA seasons. Among Hawks players, only Wilkins and Pettit averaged more points per game than Young through 2021–22. He was already among the two biggest Hawks legends.

Dominique Wilkins won his only scoring title in 1985–86 when he averaged 30.3 points per game.

HAWKS
9

CHAPTER FOUR

HAWKS MEMORIES

There was supposed to be a parade in Buffalo on November 8, 1946. Fans were there to welcome their new basketball team, the Buffalo Bisons. But rain washed out the parade. When it came to the Bisons, it turned out that many things would fail to go according to plan.

The Bisons played their first game that night. They beat the Syracuse Nationals 50–39. But the Bisons would play only a few more home games before leaving to become the Tri-Cities Blackhawks the next month.

The team finally found a home for more than a few seasons when it landed in St. Louis in 1955. That was also where the team first found real success.

The 1956–57 Hawks won their division. Winning just 34 games, they were lucky to make the playoffs. They then surprised everyone by going on a playoff run. They swept the

Bob Pettit won the NBA's first-ever MVP Award after averaging 25.7 points and 16.2 rebounds per game in 1955–56.

division rival Minneapolis Lakers in the first round. That sent them to their first NBA Finals against the Boston Celtics.

Many fans expected the Celtics would easily beat the Hawks. But St. Louis went out and won Game 1 in double overtime. The series went back and forth. In Game 6, Cliff Hagan tipped in the winning basket at the buzzer to force Game 7. That game was incredibly close. Two Bob Pettit free throws sent the game into overtime. Then a Jack Coleman bucket forced another overtime. Pettit had a shot to tie the game at the buzzer, but the Celtics won 125–123.

The Hawks improved to go 41–31 the next season. And they earned a rematch with the Celtics. Again, the Hawks won Game 1. The teams then traded wins and losses until Game 6. Boston superstar Bill Russell was limited to just 20 minutes because of injury. Hawks superstar Pettit took over. He scored 50 points as the Hawks won their first championship.

Hawks/Celtics Rivalry

The rivalry between the Hawks and the Celtics goes all the way back to 1949. At that time, the Hawks were known as the Tri-Cities Blackhawks. The rivals have met every year since, including in all four NBA Finals in which the Hawks have played.

DUNKIN' HAWKS

Dominique Wilkins and his dunking style arrived in 1982. He got the chance to show he was the best in the NBA when the

Spud Webb won the 1986 dunk contest in his hometown of Dallas.

league started holding a dunk contest in 1984. Wilkins finished third that year but was back in 1985 to win the title. The final came down to him and fellow dunking legend Michael Jordan.

The 1985 contest became best known for Jordan's dunk that started with a leap from the free-throw line. But it was Wilkins who actually took home the title. On his final dunk of the day, Wilkins wound up and slammed home a windmill jam to win the competition.

Fans couldn't wait to see Wilkins and Jordan face off again in 1986. But Jordan was injured and couldn't compete. Wilkins was there, though, as was Atlanta teammate Spud Webb.

Webb looked like an odd choice for the contest. At 5 feet, 7 inches, Webb was one of the shortest players in NBA history.

His hands weren't big enough to palm a professional-size basketball. But he could jump. He just had to jump a lot farther than Wilkins.

Webb dazzled the crowd in Dallas with 360 jams and monster slams. He threw down one jam so fiercely, the ball came down and hit his head before bouncing back through the rim. Wilkins matched Webb's breathtaking slams as the teammates dueled back and forth.

For Webb's final dunk, he stood at center court. As he entered the lane, he threw the ball with one hand at the floor. It bounced, hit the backboard, and came right back into Webb's right hand as he leaped up. He slammed it back down as the crowd went wild. Webb won the contest. He is still by far the shortest winner ever.

THE STREAK

After many disappointing seasons, the 2014–15 Hawks were enjoying a surprising run of success. The team wasn't flashy. No player averaged more than 16.7 points per game. But the team was 21–7 entering a December 26 matchup with the Milwaukee Bucks. The Hawks were blown out 107–77 that night. It was their last loss for a while.

The next night, Atlanta got revenge on Milwaukee by winning 90–85. On December 30, they beat the powerful

The Hawks had six double-digit scorers during the 2014–15 season, including Paul Millsap (4), Al Horford (15), Kyle Korver (25), and DeMarre Carroll (5).

Cleveland Cavaliers. By the time Atlanta got back home on January 7, it had won five straight games.

The wins never stopped. And they were convincing victories. Only once during Atlanta's streak did the Hawks win by fewer than five points. The biggest victory was a 120–89 demolition of the Washington Wizards on January 11.

On January 31, the Hawks defeated the Portland Trail Blazers. That was their seventeenth win of the month without a single loss. No other NBA team had ever gone 17–0 in a month. It was also the team's nineteenth win in a row. That was the sixth-longest streak in NBA history. Four Atlanta players were named to the All-Star team that year as the team won a Hawks record 60 games.

Those Hawks wound up making the Eastern Conference finals. It was the first time they had advanced that far since the playoffs went to four rounds in 1975. A few years later, a new superstar would lead them back.

Home Court

The Hawks have moved around a lot. That includes even within one city. The Hawks have had four arenas in Atlanta alone. But in 1999, they opened Philips Arena. Now State Farm Arena, it has hosted more Hawks seasons than any other building.

TIME FOR TRAE

In his first two seasons in the NBA, Trae Young established himself as a regular-season star. But NBA players are always judged by how they play when they are chasing a championship. With the Hawks struggling for wins in those two seasons, Young hadn't yet had a chance to show what he could do on the biggest stage.

The Hawks made the playoffs for the first time in Young's career in 2021. They faced the New York Knicks in the first round. The fans in New York were loud and cheered against Young all through Game 1.

The game went down to the wire. With time running out, Young dribbled around a defender. He drove to the hoop. Then he jumped and put up a high, floating shot. It dropped

Trae Young reacts to the crowd at New York's Madison Square Garden after hitting a buzzer-beating shot in Game 1 of the opening round in the 2021 Eastern Conference playoffs.

perfectly through the hoop with 0.9 seconds left. Young put his finger to his lips to quiet the crowd.

His head coach, Nate McMillan, knew the crowd would never bother his young star. "He's small, but he's a tough kid, and he's not afraid," McMillan said after the game.

The Hawks went on to win the game and the series. Young was Atlanta's leading scorer in all five games against New York. The Hawks made it all the way to the conference finals. It wasn't quite as good as a second championship. But Atlanta fans hoped that with Young leading the way, the wait would be over soon.

TIMELINE

1946

The Buffalo Bisons begin play in the National Basketball League. After playing 13 games, the team moves to the Tri-Cities area of Moline, Illinois; Rock Island, Illinois; and Davenport, Iowa, and becomes the Tri-Cities Blackhawks.

1951

After four seasons in the Tri-Cities, the Blackhawks move to Milwaukee, Wisconsin, and become known simply as the Hawks.

1955

In the team's final season in Milwaukee, Hawks forward Bob Pettit wins Rookie of the Year.

1956

Pettit wins MVP in the team's first season in St. Louis, Missouri, as the Hawks return to the playoffs for the first time since 1950.

1958

With the help of Pettit's 50 points in a decisive Game 6, the Hawks win their first NBA title over the Boston Celtics.

1968

The Hawks make one final move to Atlanta, Georgia.

1977

The Hawks are purchased by television mogul Ted Turner, who owns the team until 2001.

1982

Just over two months after he is drafted third overall by the Utah Jazz, the "Human Highlight Film" Dominique Wilkins arrives in Atlanta after a trade.

1985

Wilkins wins the NBA's dunk contest in a duel with Michael Jordan.

1986

Wilkins goes for a repeat in the dunk contest but is beaten by teammate Spud Webb, the shortest player ever to win the event.

1996

The Hawks sign future Hall of Famer Dikembe Mutombo, who goes on to win two Defensive Player of the Year awards in Atlanta.

2014

The team starts a team-record 19-game winning streak by defeating the Milwaukee Bucks 90–85 on December 27.

2015

After finishing with a losing record the year before, the Hawks win a team-record 60 games and advance past the second round of the playoffs for the first time since the playoffs expanded to four rounds in 1975.

2018

The Hawks acquire point guard Trae Young in a draft-day trade.

2021

Young and the Hawks return to the playoffs and advance to the conference finals.

TEAM FACTS

FRANCHISE HISTORY

Buffalo Bisons (1946)
Tri-Cities Blackhawks (1947–51)
Milwaukee Hawks (1951–55)
St. Louis Hawks (1955–68)
Atlanta Hawks (1968–)

NBA CHAMPIONSHIPS

1958

KEY PLAYERS

Mookie Blaylock (1992–99)
John Drew (1974–82)
Al Horford (2007–16)
Lou Hudson (1966–77)
Pete Maravich (1970–74)
Dikembe Mutombo (1996–2001)
Bob Pettit (1954–65)
Wayne Rollins (1977–88)
Lenny Wilkens (1960–68)
Dominique Wilkins (1982–94)
Trae Young (2018–)

KEY COACHES

Mike Fratello (1981, 1983–90)
Alex Hannum (1956–58)
Lenny Wilkens (1993–2000)

HOME ARENAS

Buffalo Memorial Auditorium (1946)
Wharton Field House (1946–51)
Milwaukee Arena (1951–55)
Kiel Auditorium/St. Louis Arena (1955–68)
Alexander Memorial Coliseum (1968–72, 1997–99)
Omni Coliseum (1972–97)
Georgia Dome (1997–99)
State Farm Arena (1999–)
Formerly known as:
Philips Arena (1999–2018)

TEAM TRIVIA

DUNKING AGAIN

In 2005 Atlanta rookie forward Josh Smith joined Dominique Wilkins and Spud Webb as a dunk contest winner. He became the fifth player to record three perfect scores in one contest. One of the other four was Webb during his win in 1986.

ONE-GAME WONDER

All-Star Rasheed Wallace played 16 NBA seasons with six different teams. One of those was Atlanta—and for only one game. The Hawks traded for Wallace in February 2004, and he scored 20 points in a loss to the New Jersey Nets. Wallace was then traded again to the Detroit Pistons, where he played the rest of the season.

AGE IS JUST A NUMBER

On March 4, 2019, Hawks forward Vince Carter scored 21 points by hitting seven three-pointers against the Miami Heat. Carter was 42 years, 37 days old, making him the oldest player ever to top 20 points in an NBA game.

THE ONE THAT GOT AWAY

NBA legend Bob Cousy was originally drafted by the Tri-Cities Blackhawks in 1950. But Cousy, a native of Massachusetts, did not want to play so far from home. He ended up with the Boston Celtics and led the NBA in assists eight times during his Hall-of-Fame career.

GLOSSARY

assist
A pass that leads directly to a basket.

draft
A system that allows teams to acquire new players coming into a league.

era
A period of time in history.

overtime
An extra period of play when the score is tied after regulation.

rebounding
Catching the ball after a shot has been missed.

rookie
A professional athlete in his or her first year of competition.

roster
A list of players who make up a team.

steal
To take the ball from a player on the other team.

swept
Won every game in a series.

veteran
A player who has played many years.

MORE
INFORMATION

BOOKS

Graves, Will. *NBA*. Minneapolis, MN: Abdo Publishing, 2021.

Mahoney, Brian. *GOATs of Basketball*. Minneapolis, MN: Abdo Publishing, 2022.

Mason, Tyler. *Ultimate NBA Road Trip*. Minneapolis, MN: Abdo Publishing, 2019.

ONLINE RESOURCES

Booklinks
NONFICTION NETWORK
FREE! ONLINE NONFICTION RESOURCES

To learn more about the Atlanta Hawks, please visit **abdobooklinks.com** or scan this QR code. These links are routinely monitored and updated to provide the most current information available.

INDEX

ABOUT THE AUTHOR

Anthony K. Hewson is a freelance writer originally from San Diego. He and his wife now live in the San Francisco Bay Area with their two dogs.